THE ART AND SCIENCE OF PHISHING

UNDERSTANDING, PREVENTING, AND RESPONDING

Dr. Karthik Karunakaran, Ph.D.

Printed in the United States of America.

For more information, or to book an event, contact :
karthikk@alumni.iitm.ac.in

CONTENTS

CHAPTER 1

THE ANATOMY OF DECEPTION: UNDERSTANDING THE PERSISTENT THREAT OF PHISHING IN THE DIGITAL AGE

In the labyrinth of the internet, where opportunity and danger coexist in equal measure, phishing emerges as a dark art —a sophisticated dance of deception and trust manipulation. Originating in the 1990s as an offshoot of early hacking culture, phishing is a testament to the ingenuity of malice cloaked in familiarity. Over time, it has evolved into a pervasive cyber threat, exploiting the vulnerabilities of human psychology and the intricacies of digital ecosystems. To understand why phishing remains so potent, we must journey through its origins, dissect its psychological underpinnings, and explore its ever-adaptive nature.

Origins and Evolution: A Brief Historical Overview

Phishing's roots trace back to the dawn of widespread internet adoption. The term is a play on "fishing," where bait lures the unsuspecting victim. Early attackers, often rogue hackers, targeted America Online (AOL) users, crafting fraudulent messages that mimicked official communications. The simplicity of these attempts belied their effectiveness; users, unfamiliar with digital threats, often fell prey to requests for passwords and financial details.

As the internet matured, so did phishing. By the 2000s, email became a fertile ground for scams, with attackers deploying more sophisticated tactics. Today, phishing spans a spectrum of mediums—SMS ("smishing"), voice calls ("vishing"), and even social media. The advent of artificial intelligence has further amplified the threat, enabling cybercriminals to personalise attacks at scale, making their schemes alarmingly convincing.

The Psychology of Phishing: Why It Works

Phishing's success lies in its exploitation of human psychology. At its core, it leverages principles that govern trust, fear, and urgency:

1. Authority and Trust: People are conditioned to comply with perceived authority figures, whether a bank, employer, or government entity. Phishers often impersonate such entities, relying on logos, tone, and professional language to lend credibility.

2. Fear and Urgency: Messages threatening dire consequences—account suspension, legal action, or financial loss—evoke fear and compel hasty decisions. This sense of urgency bypasses critical thinking, leaving victims vulnerable.

3. Greed and Curiosity: The promise of a reward—a

lottery win, exclusive offer, or secret opportunity—appeals to innate desires, luring individuals to click on malicious links.

4. Cognitive Overload: In a world saturated with information, people often operate on autopilot, skimming through emails and texts. Phishers exploit this inattention, embedding their traps in seemingly innocuous communications.

The Adaptive Nature of Phishing: Staying Ahead of Defenses

What makes phishing especially insidious is its adaptability. As organisations deploy sophisticated cybersecurity measures, phishers evolve their tactics. Spear-phishing, a targeted variation, exemplifies this evolution, using personalised information from social media or public records to craft convincing attacks. Advanced Persistent Threat (APT) groups, often state-sponsored, deploy phishing as a precursor to espionage, targeting high-value individuals and organisations.

Moreover, the proliferation of deepfake technology and AI-generated content adds a chilling dimension. Imagine receiving a voice message from a trusted colleague or a video call from your boss, only to discover it was a synthetic manipulation. Such scenarios are no longer confined to speculative fiction but are active threats in the digital landscape.

The Human Factor: A Double-Edged Sword

Despite technological advancements, humans remain the weakest link—and paradoxically, the most vigorous defence. Cybersecurity education and awareness programs have proven effective in mitigating risks. However, the dynamic nature of phishing requires constant vigilance. It's a battle of wits where technology alone cannot suffice; emotional intelligence, scepticism, and proactive behaviour are critical.

Emotional Resonance: Why This Matters

Phishing is not just a technological problem; it is a human tragedy. The financial and emotional toll on victims can be devastating—savings lost, identities stolen, and trust shattered. Organisations face reputational damage, legal repercussions, and operational disruptions. Yet, the fight against phishing is not hopeless. Each informed individual represents a bulwark against deception, a beacon of resilience in the face of cunning adversaries.

CHAPTER 2

THE ART OF DECEPTION: A COMPREHENSIVE EXAMINATION OF PHISHING METHODS IN THE DIGITAL AGE

Phishing, the artful con lurking in the digital world's shadows, is as old as the internet itself. Yet, its tactics and tools are constantly evolving, adapting to the rhythms of our interconnected lives. At its core, phishing exploits trust—an invaluable and perilous human trait in cyberspace.

Email Phishing: The Gateway to Deception

Email phishing is the progenitor of modern phishing techniques, combining simplicity with devastating effectiveness. The modus operandi is straightforward: a crafted email masquerades as a legitimate entity—a bank, e-commerce platform, or employer— requesting sensitive information or prompting the recipient to click a malicious link.

Despite decades of awareness campaigns, email phishing continues to thrive. The reasons are manifold: sheer volume, increasingly sophisticated designs, and exploiting human emotions like fear or greed. These emails often use urgency as a weapon—"Your account will be suspended unless you act now!"—short-circuiting critical thinking in favour of reflexive compliance.

Spear Phishing: Precision in Manipulation

While email phishing casts a wide net, spear phishing takes a sniper's approach. Tailored to specific individuals or organisations, spear phishing leverages publicly available information to craft highly personalised attacks. To establish credibility, a criminal might research a company executive's LinkedIn profile, referencing their recent keynote or professional achievements.

The stakes here are higher, as spear phishing often targets high-value individuals—CEOs, government officials, or IT administrators. The consequences? Stolen intellectual property, compromised systems, and reputational damage that can take years to repair.

Vishing: Voices of Deception

Phishing transcends the written word with vishing or voice phishing. Here, attackers use phone calls to manipulate victims into divulging sensitive information. Impersonating authority figures—such as tax officials, law enforcement, or technical support representatives—they weave narratives designed to incite panic or urgency.

Consider a victim receiving a call claiming unpaid taxes, which will result in an arrest unless payment is made immediately. The voice on the line may be calm and professional or deliberately stern, exploiting psychological pressure points. The shift toward mobile-first communications has only bolstered Vishing's reach, making it a formidable threat.

Smishing: The Subtle Stinger

Smishing, or SMS phishing, epitomises the adage that less is more. Short text messages, purporting to be from trusted sources, direct recipients to click links or reply with personal details. The messages often play on common fears or desires: a missed package delivery, a security alert from your bank, or an offer too good to refuse.

Unlike emails, text messages often bypass spam filters, landing directly in the victim's inbox. Their brevity makes them seem innocuous, yet their consequences can be anything but. The rise of mobile-first lifestyles amplifies smishing's impact, turning a ubiquitous tool of convenience into an exploitation channel.

Social Media Scams: Breeding Grounds for Trust

Social media platforms, where connections are built and trust is cultivated, have become fertile grounds for phishing attacks. Scammers exploit these digital communities to lure victims through fake profiles, fraudulent giveaways, or direct messages.

One common tactic is the "help request" scam: an attacker, posing as a friend or acquaintance, claims they are stranded and need financial assistance. Alternatively, fake job offers promise lucrative opportunities, baiting victims into sharing personal or financial information.

The intersection of social media and phishing highlights a chilling reality: in a world where we share so much, our digital identities can be weaponised against us.

The Evolving Threat: New Frontiers in Phishing

Phishing is not static; it evolves with technological advancements and societal shifts. The integration of artificial intelligence enables attackers to craft increasingly convincing messages, mimicking human language and tone with unsettling precision. Deepfakes, combining synthetic audio and video, add a terrifying dimension where a trusted colleague or loved one might appear to ask for help.

The COVID-19 pandemic saw an explosion of phishing attempts as criminals capitalised on fear and uncertainty. Fake vaccine registration links, fraudulent stimulus check portals, and counterfeit charity appeals flooded inboxes and phones, preying on humanity's collective vulnerability.

The Emotional Toll: Beyond Financial Loss

While phishing's financial repercussions are well-documented —billions of dollars lost annually—the emotional toll on victims often goes unspoken. For individuals, falling prey to a phishing scam can evoke shame, guilt, and distrust. Organisations, meanwhile, grapple with eroded employee morale and reputational damage.

Yet, amidst the chaos, there is resilience. Awareness campaigns, training programs, and community efforts have empowered individuals and institutions to recognise and combat phishing attempts. The growing emphasis on cybersecurity education is a testament to the human spirit's capacity for adaptation.

CHAPTER 3

ANATOMY OF DECEPTION: DISSECTING THE KEY ELEMENTS OF A PHISHING EMAIL

In the digital jungle, where convenience and communication thrive, the phishing email lurks as a predator, ready to ensnare the unsuspecting. Cloaked in an illusion of legitimacy, phishing emails exploit human trust and technological loopholes with devastating precision.

The Subject Line: Bait on the Hook

A phishing email begins its assault the moment it arrives in your inbox. Like a well-crafted headline, its subject line is designed to grab your attention and provoke a reaction. These lines often employ tactics such as urgency, fear, or curiosity.

Examples include:

- "Urgent: Your Account Will Be Locked in 24 Hours!"
- "Final Notice: Unusual Activity Detected in Your Account"
- "Congratulations! You've Won a $1,000 Gift Card!"

Each subject line plays on emotions that bypass critical thinking, compelling recipients to open the email immediately. In the age of instant communication, the mere thought of missing out or facing a dire consequence is enough to make even the most cautious individual click.

Manipulated Sender Details: The Illusion of Trust

The sender's email address is the second element in this elaborate con. Phishers often manipulate these details to mimic legitimate entities, relying on slight alterations that are easy to miss. For example:

- Legitimate: support@bank.com
- Fake: support@bank-secure.com

Sophisticated attackers may use spoofing to make the email appear as though it originates from an authentic address. This manipulation leverages the trust people place in known brands or institutions. Recognising this deception requires vigilance—hovering over the sender's name to reveal the underlying email address often exposes fraud.

The Greeting: Personalisation as a Weapon

A hallmark of phishing emails is their greeting—or lack thereof. Generic salutations such as "Dear Customer" or "Dear User" are common in older phishing attempts. However, modern phishers employ personalisation to enhance credibility by addressing the recipient by name or referencing specific details from prior data breaches or social media profiles.

This personal touch tricks victims into lowering their guard, as the email appears tailored rather than mass-produced. Yet, this veneer of familiarity often betrays its true intent.

The Body: A Symphony of Manipulation

The body of a phishing email is where the deception unfolds in full. Every sentence is crafted to evoke urgency, fear, or a sense of obligation. The content often includes:

- Threats of Consequences: "Your account will be permanently disabled if you do not respond within 48 hours."
- Appeals to authority: "As per our security team's recommendation, immediate action is required."
- Offers Too Good to Be True: "Claim your exclusive reward by clicking the link below."

Formatting plays a critical role here. Phishers use logos, fonts, and layouts that mimic official communications, exploiting our familiarity with legitimate branding. Typos and grammatical errors, once a giveaway, are now less common as attackers refine their techniques.

The Call to Action: The Moment of Truth

At the heart of every phishing email lies a call to action—a demand for the recipient to do something, whether clicking a link, downloading an attachment, or providing sensitive information.

Malicious Links: Often disguised as hyperlinks like "Verify Now" or "Reset Password," these links redirect users to fake websites designed to steal credentials. Hovering over the link to reveal the URL is a critical defence tactic.

Attachments: PDFs, Word documents, or ZIP files are frequently used to deliver malware. These files may contain macros or embedded scripts that execute malicious code upon opening.

The Signature: Legitimacy at the Finish Line

The closing signature attempts to reinforce the illusion of

authenticity. It might include:

- A formal sign-off, such as "Sincerely, Customer Support Team."
- Contact details that mimic real addresses or phone numbers.
- Disclaimers about security ironically emphasise the importance of not sharing personal information.

Including these elements disarms scepticism, making the email appear more genuine and professional.

Psychological Triggers: Why They Work

Phishing emails succeed because they exploit fundamental psychological principles:

- Fear: Threats of account suspension or legal consequences induce panic, leading to rash decisions.
- Curiosity: Unusual subjects or mysterious offers pique interest, prompting clicks.
- Authority: Messages from "trusted" entities, like banks or employers, leverage our tendency to comply with perceived authority figures.
- FOMO (Fear of Missing Out): Promises of exclusive offers or urgent deadlines tap into the fear of losing opportunities.

The Evolving Threat: Staying Ahead of the Curve

Phishing emails have become more sophisticated, employing advanced techniques like AI-generated content and dynamic phishing kits that adapt to victims' interactions. Attackers use real-time feedback to refine their approaches, ensuring higher success rates.

For example, some phishing emails incorporate CAPTCHA

challenges or SSL certificates on fake sites to appear more legitimate. These tactics blur the line between genuine and fraudulent, making vigilance and education all the more critical.

CHAPTER 4

THE FACADE OF TRUST: AN IN-DEPTH ANALYSIS OF FAKE WEBSITES AND THE ART OF DIGITAL DECEPTION

In the sprawling ecosystem of the internet, where trust and utility define our interactions, cybercriminals wield one of the most insidious tools in their arsenal: the fake website. These digital forgeries, meticulously designed to mimic trusted brands, serve as gateways to fraud, identity theft, and data breaches. They are masterpieces of manipulation, crafted to exploit human behaviour and technological blind spots.

The Illusion of Authenticity: Crafting Convincing Designs

At first glance, a fake website often appears indistinguishable from its legitimate counterpart. This visual fidelity is no accident; it results from deliberate efforts to replicate every element of a trusted brand's online presence. From logos and colour schemes to fonts and layouts, cybercriminals meticulously study their target to ensure their counterfeit appear genuine.

1. Visual Cloning: Criminals use screenshots, open-source tools, or even direct copies of HTML and CSS to replicate the exact design of a legitimate website. Familiarity breeds trust, and a user landing on such a site may feel immediately at ease.

2. Domain Spoofing: A fake website's web address is often crafted to mimic a legitimate domain, with slight alterations that can easily escape notice. Examples include:

    - Substituting characters: www.amaz0n.com (using a zero instead of an "o").
    - Adding extra words: www.bank-login-secure.com.
    - Exploiting internationalised domain names (IDNs): using non-Latin characters to mimic Latin ones.

3. Secure Appearances: Many fake websites now display HTTPS and padlock icons, leveraging users' perception that these indicators guarantee legitimacy. This misconception emboldens criminals, as victims often fail to scrutinise other signs of authenticity.

The Psychological Blueprint: Exploiting Human Behavior

The success of fake websites hinges not only on their technical design but also on their ability to exploit psychological triggers. Cybercriminals are masters of behavioural manipulation, tapping into emotions and instincts that cloud judgment.

1. Urgency and Fear: Fake websites often present alarming messages such as "Your account has been compromised" or "Act now to avoid suspension." These

prompts create a sense of urgency that overrides critical thinking.

2. Authority and Trust: Cybercriminals leverage the authority these entities command by imitating well-known brands or institutions—banks, government agencies, or tech companies. Users are conditioned to trust such sources, making them less likely to question the website's legitimacy.

3. Convenience and Desire: Fake e-commerce websites lure victims with incredible deals, limited-time offers, or hard-to-find products. The prospect of securing a bargain often blinds users to the risks, leading them to enter payment details without verifying the site's authenticity.

The Mechanics of Deception: How Fake Websites Steal Data

Once a victim interacts with a fake website, the mechanisms of theft come into play. These methods are as diverse as they are malicious, reflecting the ingenuity of cybercriminals.

1. Credential Harvesting: Login forms on fake websites collect usernames and passwords, which criminals use to access accounts or sell on the dark web. Many victims unknowingly reuse passwords, compounding the damage.

2. Financial Fraud: Fake payment portals capture credit card details, enabling unauthorised transactions. Sometimes, the fake website might process a small, seemingly legitimate purchase to avoid immediate detection.

3. Malware Distribution: Fake websites often serve as

conduits for malware, embedding malicious scripts that activate upon clicking links or downloading files. These programs can steal additional data, monitor keystrokes, or hijack entire systems.

4. Phishing as a Gateway: Some fake websites act as phishing launchpads, redirecting victims to other fraudulent pages or initiating further attempts to gather sensitive information.

Technological Tactics: Tools of the Trade

Building and maintaining fake websites require technical expertise and an arsenal of tools. Cybercriminals often rely on publicly available resources and infrastructure to streamline their operations.

1. Phishing Kits: These prepackaged toolkits include templates, scripts, and instructions for creating fake websites. Sold on dark web marketplaces, they enable even novice attackers to execute convincing scams.

2. Automation: Bots and scripts help cybercriminals deploy and manage multiple fake websites simultaneously, maximising their reach while minimising effort.

3. Dynamic Content: Advanced fake websites use dynamic elements to adapt based on user input or device type, enhancing their realism. For example, a phoney banking site might display a personalised greeting based on stolen data.

4. Bulletproof Hosting: To avoid takedown attempts, criminals often use hosting services in jurisdictions with lax regulations or rely on decentralised platforms

like the Tor network.

The Evolution of Fake Websites: Adapting to Defense Mechanisms

As awareness and cybersecurity defences improve, fake websites continue to evolve. The integration of AI allows for hyper-realistic designs and adaptive interactions, while deepfake technology introduces new dimensions of deception.

Recent trends include:

- Mobile Optimisation: Recognising the dominance of smartphones, fake websites are increasingly designed to perform flawlessly on mobile browsers.
- Localised Content: Cybercriminals now tailor fake websites to specific regions, using local languages, currencies, and cultural references to enhance credibility.
- Real-Time Feedback: Some fake websites mimic genuine login processes, using stolen credentials to test and validate accounts in real-time.

The Cost of Deception: Beyond Monetary Losses

The impact of fake websites extends far beyond financial losses. For individuals, the theft of personal data leads to identity fraud, emotional distress, and years of damage control. Organisations, meanwhile, face reputational harm, legal liabilities, and the erosion of customer trust.

The emotional toll on victims is profound. Discovering that you've been deceived can evoke shame and betrayal, discouraging individuals from reporting incidents. This silence allows cybercriminals to continue their operations unabated.

Building Resilience: A Path Forward

The fight against fake websites requires a multifaceted approach:

- Education and Awareness: Teaching users to scrutinise URLs, verify website authenticity, and avoid clicking on unsolicited links is crucial.
- Technological Defenses: Organisations must invest in anti-phishing tools, two-factor authentication, and domain monitoring to protect customers.
- Collective Action: Governments, tech companies, and cybersecurity firms must collaborate to dismantle phishing networks and prosecute offenders.

CHAPTER 5

THE HUMAN ELEMENT: HOW PSYCHOLOGICAL TACTICS DRIVE PHISHING SUCCESS

In the grand theatre of cybercrime, phishing is a performance perfected through psychological manipulation. It thrives not on technological prowess alone but on exploiting the intricate vulnerabilities of human psychology. Fear, urgency, curiosity, and trust—the cardinal emotions and instincts that guide human behaviour—become weapons in the phisher's arsenal.

Fear: The Currency of Control

Fear is one of humanity's most primal emotions, and phishers wield it like a scalpel. By triggering anxiety and panic, they compel victims to act without critical thought. Phishing emails often convey alarming messages, such as:

- "Your account has been compromised."

- "Suspicious activity detected—verify immediately to avoid suspension."

- "IRS audit notice: Immediate response required."

The urgency to avoid negative consequences creates a mental tunnel vision, where the recipient focuses solely on resolving the apparent crisis. In such moments, the ability to assess the email's authenticity diminishes, and clicking a malicious link is the only logical choice.

Case in Point: During tax season, phishing scams claiming to be from revenue agencies skyrocket. Fear of audits or penalties makes these emails particularly effective, especially against individuals unfamiliar with government protocols.

Urgency: The Thief of Rationality

Phishing exploits the human tendency to prioritise immediate action over careful deliberation when time appears to be running out. Messages like "Respond within 24 hours" or "Offer expires soon" create a sense of scarcity, borrowing principles from sales and marketing to manipulate behaviour.

This tactic relies on a psychological phenomenon called temporal discounting, where people value immediate outcomes more than long-term considerations. Faced with a ticking clock, victims often bypass their usual scepticism to avoid missing out or incurring a penalty.

Example: A phishing email from a "bank" warning of an impending account freeze often includes a countdown timer or specific deadline. These artificial constraints intensify the urgency, pressuring the recipient into swift and uninformed action.

Curiosity: The Key to Engagement

Curiosity is a double-edged sword—a driver of innovation and a vulnerability waiting to be exploited. Phishing campaigns leverage curiosity through vague or enticing subject lines designed to provoke clicks:

- "You won't believe what happens next!"
- "Exclusive offer just for you!"
- "See the photos from last night!"

These tactics play on the brain's reward system, which is wired to seek answers to unresolved questions. The ambiguity or intrigue in these messages overrides caution, leading victims to engage with the email and its malicious payload.

Modern Twist: Social media has amplified curiosity-driven phishing. Messages like "Who viewed your profile?" or fake notifications about tagged photos exploit the innate desire to know what others think or say about us.

Trust: The Illusion of Legitimacy

Trust is the cornerstone of phishing success. By impersonating authority figures or familiar brands, phishers manipulate victims into believing the authenticity of their requests. Emails from "banks," "employers," or "government agencies" carry an inherent credibility that discourages scrutiny.

Phishers enhance this illusion by mimicking the following:

- Official logos, language, and formatting.
- Personalisation, addressing victims by name or referencing specific details.
- Domain names that closely resemble legitimate ones (e.g., paypal-secure.com).

This tactic preys on the human tendency to defer to perceived authority figures, a psychological principle outlined by sociologist Stanley Milgram. When instructions come from a trusted source, people are more likely to comply without question.

Real-World Scenario: In business email compromise (BEC) scams, attackers impersonate CEOs or financial officers, instructing employees to transfer funds or share sensitive information. The inherent trust in authority makes such scams devastatingly effective.

The Cognitive Shortcut: Why It Works

At the heart of phishing's success lies the brain's reliance on heuristics—mental shortcuts used to make quick decisions. While heuristics are essential for navigating a complex world, they can lead to errors when exploited by skilled manipulators.

1. Availability Heuristic: Victims recall recent warnings about fraud or security issues and assume the phishing email aligns with legitimate concerns.

2. Social Proof: Messages claiming "Thousands have already benefited" tap into the desire to conform to what others are doing.

3. Reciprocity: Fake offers or rewards create a psychological obligation to "return the favour" by complying with the request.

These shortcuts save cognitive effort but make individuals susceptible to well-crafted deceptions.

Emotional Resonance: The Aftermath of Deception

Phishing doesn't merely steal data; it leaves psychological scars. Victims often feel a profound sense of shame and betrayal, questioning their judgment and competence. This emotional fallout can deter individuals from reporting the crime, further empowering cyber criminals.

Phishers understand these emotional dynamics and craft their tactics to capitalise on them:

- Victims of fear-based phishing are less likely to admit they acted impulsively.

- Trust-based scams exploit the very relationships people rely on for security and reassurance.

The emotional toll of phishing underscores the need for empathetic responses and robust education to prevent such attacks.

The Evolving Landscape: Staying One Step Ahead

As awareness of phishing tactics grows, so does the sophistication of these schemes. Artificial intelligence enables attackers to create hyper-personalised messages, while deepfake technology can mimic voices or videos to enhance trust. In this evolving battle, understanding psychological manipulation remains our most vigorous defence.

1. Behavioural Training: Teaching individuals to recognise and resist emotional triggers in phishing attempts.

2. Technological Tools: AI-driven filters that detect and block phishing emails based on patterns and context.

3. Cultural Shifts: Encouraging open discussions about phishing to reduce stigma and increase reporting.

CHAPTER 6

THE ART OF PRECISION: DECODING THE PERSONALISATION AND THREAT OF SPEAR PHISHING

In the digital realm, where connectivity is both a strength and vulnerability, spear phishing emerges as a surgical strike in cybercriminals' arsenal. Unlike the broad net cast by traditional phishing, spear phishing is a scalpel meticulously designed to exploit precise details about individuals or organisations.

The Anatomy of Spear Phishing: A Masterclass in Deception

Spear phishing derives its potency from one defining characteristic: personalisation. By leveraging specific information about a target, attackers craft messages that resonate on a deeply personal level, disarming scepticism and increasing the likelihood of success. The sophistication of these attacks lies not only in their technical execution but in their psychological acumen.

1. Research and Reconnaissance: Cybercriminals begin by gathering detailed information about their target through a variety of means:

    - Social Media: Public profiles like LinkedIn, Facebook, or Instagram reveal job titles, hobbies, connections, and recent activities.

    - Corporate Websites: Organisational hierarchies, email conventions, and ongoing projects provide context for crafting believable narratives.

    - Data Breaches: Compromised credentials from previous leaks offer valuable starting points for tailoring attacks.

2. Personalised Communication: Armed with this data, attackers create emails, messages, or calls that feel authentic. These often include:

    - Specific names, positions, or project details.

    - References to recent events or shared experiences.

    - A tone or style mirroring the target's known preferences or professional culture.

Precision in Execution: What Sets Spear Phishing Apart

The hallmark of spear phishing is its ability to bypass generic suspicion by appearing as part of the victim's everyday digital interactions. The tactics employed reflect an almost artistic dedication to believability:

1. Impersonation: Attackers often pose as trusted colleagues, superiors, or business partners. For example:
   - An email seemingly from a CEO requesting an urgent wire transfer.
   - The "IT department" message instructs the recipient to reset their password.

2. Contextual Relevance: By incorporating timely and specific details, spear phishing messages align perfectly with the target's ongoing concerns. A marketing executive might receive a fake invoice from a well-known vendor, while an HR manager could be tricked into opening a resume loaded with malware.

3. Dynamic Adaptation: Some attacks use real-time interactions to enhance credibility. For instance, attackers may engage in email exchanges, gradually building trust before delivering their malicious payload.

Psychological Manipulation: Turning Knowledge into Exploitation

Spear phishing thrives on its ability to manipulate human psychology. These attacks bypass even the most cautious individuals by appealing to emotions and leveraging trust.

1. Urgency and Authority: Emails that demand

immediate action, especially when seemingly from a superior, capitalise on the pressure to comply. Victims often prioritise the perceived importance of the request over verifying its legitimacy.

2. Trust and Familiarity: Spear phishing messages exploit the inherent trust in known relationships. A "trusted colleague" request to share sensitive data feels natural, especially if it aligns with ongoing conversations.

3. Greed and Opportunity: Promises of exclusive deals, job offers, or financial incentives appeal to the target's aspirations. When combined with a personalised touch, such lures become almost irresistible.

Real-World Implications: The High Stakes of Precision

The impact of spear phishing is felt across industries and sectors, often with catastrophic consequences:

1. Corporate Espionage: Attackers use spear phishing to infiltrate companies, stealing intellectual property, trade secrets, or competitive intelligence. The precision of these attacks ensures access to critical personnel and systems.

2. Financial Fraud: High-value spear phishing

campaigns, such as business email compromise (BEC) scams, have cost organisations billions globally. By impersonating executives or vendors, attackers orchestrate fraudulent transactions with alarming efficiency.

3. National Security Risks: Government agencies and critical infrastructure are prime targets. Spear phishing has been used to gain access to classified information, disrupt operations, and conduct surveillance.

Notable Case: In 2016, spear phishing played a pivotal role in the breach of a major U.S. political party, resulting in leaked emails that influenced public discourse and demonstrated the far-reaching consequences of targeted attacks.

The Evolution of Spear Phishing: Riding the Waves of Technology

As technology advances, so too does the sophistication of spear phishing. Artificial intelligence (AI) and machine learning (ML) are reshaping the landscape, enabling attackers to scale and refine their campaigns:

1. AI-Driven Personalization: AI tools analyse vast datasets to create hyper-personalised messages, mimicking the tone, style, and behaviour of real individuals.

2. Deepfake Integration: Video and audio deepfakes add a new dimension to impersonation, making it increasingly difficult to discern genuine communications from fabrications.

3. Automation with Precision: While spear phishing was traditionally labour-intensive, automation now allows attackers to execute multiple targeted campaigns simultaneously without sacrificing quality.

Defensive Strategies: Strengthening the Human Firewall

The battle against spear phishing requires a blend of technological defences and human vigilance:

1. Awareness and Training: Educating employees and individuals about spear phishing tactics is paramount. Recognising red flags, such as unexpected requests for sensitive information or unusual communication patterns, can thwart attacks.

2. Technological Safeguards: Advanced email filters, multi-factor authentication (MFA), and endpoint detection tools can mitigate risks. AI-driven anomaly detection systems are increasingly effective at identifying suspicious activities.

3. Fostering a Culture of Verification: Encouraging individuals to verify requests through independent channels—such as phone calls or in-person confirmations—can prevent falling prey to impersonation.

CHAPTER 7

THE DOMINO EFFECT: HOW PHISHING ATTACKS DISRUPT BUSINESSES

In the intricate ecosystem of modern commerce, trust is the invisible currency that powers transactions, partnerships, and innovation. Yet, phishing attacks—those calculated acts of deception—threaten to erode this trust, disrupting businesses profoundly and often irrevocably. These cyberattacks, seemingly innocuous in their simplicity, wield an outsized impact on financial stability, data security, and brand reputation.

The Anatomy of a Disruption: Financial Losses

At the heart of phishing's menace is its ability to siphon financial resources directly and indirectly from businesses. The costs are not limited to stolen funds; they extend to remediation efforts, lost productivity, and regulatory penalties.

1. Direct Theft: Business email compromise (BEC) scams—an advanced form of phishing

—have become a lucrative enterprise for cybercriminals. Attackers orchestrate fraudulent transactions by impersonating executives or vendors, often draining millions from unsuspecting companies.

Case in Point: In 2019, a European aerospace company fell victim to a spear-phishing attack that cost them over $240 million. The attacker posed as a trusted supplier, redirecting payments to a fraudulent account.

2. Incident Response and Recovery: Once a phishing attack is detected, businesses must invest heavily in damage control:

- Forensic investigations to identify vulnerabilities.

- Cybersecurity upgrades to prevent future breaches.

- Legal fees to address potential liabilities and compliance violations.

These efforts drain resources that could otherwise be allocated to growth and innovation.

3. Regulatory Fines: A phishing-induced data breach can result in hefty fines in sectors governed by strict data protection laws like finance or healthcare. Non-compliance with regulations like the GDPR or HIPAA compounds the financial burden.

The Fallout of Data Breaches: More Than Numbers

Phishing attacks frequently serve as the entry point for data breaches, exposing sensitive information that underpins a business's operations. The implications of such breaches are far-reaching:

1. Intellectual Property Theft: For companies in innovation-driven industries, the loss of trade secrets or proprietary data can devastate their competitive edge. Attackers may sell this information to competitors or use it to sabotage future projects.

2. Customer and Employee Data Exposure: Compromising personal data erodes trust among customers and employees. Victims of identity theft, credit fraud, or harassment often hold the breached company accountable, leading to legal actions and reputational damage.

3. Operational Disruption: In some cases, phishing facilitates ransomware attacks, paralysing critical systems until a ransom is paid. Downtime caused by such attacks results in lost revenue and productivity, with ripple effects throughout the supply chain.

The Intangible Cost: Brand Reputation

While financial losses can be quantified and data breaches eventually mitigated, damaging a brand's reputation is more challenging to repair. Trust, once broken, is not quickly rebuilt.

1. Erosion of Customer Loyalty: Customers entrust businesses with their data, expecting it to be safeguarded. A phishing-related breach shatters this expectation, prompting customers to seek alternatives. The loss of loyal patrons can have a lasting impact on revenue streams.

2. Negative Publicity: Media coverage of phishing attacks often paints a picture of negligence or incompetence, tarnishing a company's public image. Even businesses with strong security practices can struggle to shake the stigma of being "hacked."

3. Impact on Partnerships: Companies implicated in phishing attacks may find maintaining partnerships challenging or attracting new collaborators challenging. The perception of vulnerability makes them less appealing to stakeholders seeking stability and security.

Ripple Effects: Beyond the Immediate Victim

The repercussions of phishing attacks extend beyond the targeted business, affecting the broader ecosystem in which it operates.

1. Supply Chain Vulnerabilities: When a supplier or vendor is compromised, the fallout can cascade to their partners. For example, a phishing attack on a logistics provider can disrupt deliveries for multiple clients, amplifying the economic impact.

2. Industry-Wide Consequences: High-profile phishing incidents in one organisation often trigger increased scrutiny across the entire industry. Competitors may face stricter regulations or heightened customer scepticism, even if they are not directly affected.

3. National and Global Implications: In critical sectors such as finance, energy, or healthcare, phishing attacks can have geopolitical ramifications. The theft of sensitive data or disruption of essential services poses risks to national security and economic stability.

A Wake-Up Call: Why Phishing Remains a Potent Threat

Despite advancements in cybersecurity, phishing continues to thrive due to its adaptability and reliance on human error. The democratisation of phishing kits on the dark web has made these attacks accessible to even novice cybercriminals, while artificial intelligence enables the creation of increasingly convincing deceptions.

The evolving nature of phishing underscores the need for businesses to adopt a proactive approach:

- Employee Training: Regular awareness programs can empower employees to recognise and report phishing attempts.

- Advanced Detection Systems: AI-driven tools can identify and neutralise phishing emails before they reach their targets.

- Comprehensive Incident Plans: Businesses must develop and regularly update response plans to minimise the damage of successful attacks.

CHAPTER 8

THE SUBTLE ART OF DECEPTION: PHISHING IN CYBER ESPIONAGE CAMPAIGNS

Phishing has emerged as an unparalleled weapon of choice in the shadowy corridors of espionage, where secrets are the most coveted currency. Its simplicity belies its potency, offering cybercriminals and nation-states a covert means to infiltrate governments and corporations. This essay explores how phishing is weaponised in cyber espionage campaigns, unravelling the layers of deception that make it a formidable tool. Through an incisive lens, we examine its tactics, implications, and evolving strategies to counter this pervasive threat.

Phishing as a Gateway to Espionage

Phishing is the silent infiltrator, slipping through digital defences by exploiting human vulnerabilities. Unlike brute-force hacking, which relies on technical prowess, phishing operates in the psychological domain, manipulating trust and curiosity. Cyber espionage becomes a precision instrument to extract sensitive data, compromise critical systems, and sow discord.

1. Reconnaissance and Targeting:

Espionage-oriented phishing campaigns begin with meticulous research. Attackers identify key individuals—often high-ranking officials, executives, or IT personnel—whose access can be the gateway to classified information. Social media profiles, corporate directories, and leaked datasets provide many exploitable details.

For example, an attacker targeting a government agency might pose as a foreign diplomat, sending a carefully crafted email referencing a recent international summit. The veneer of authenticity disarms suspicion, prompting the recipient to engage.

2. Tailored Deceptions:

Espionage phishing eschews generic messages in favour of tailored narratives that align with the target's professional context. Tactics include:

- Malicious Attachments: Disguised as innocuous reports or meeting minutes, these files deliver malware upon opening.

- Credential Harvesting: Links lead to counterfeit login portals, capturing usernames and passwords that grant attackers access to secure networks.

- Trojanized Updates: Fake software updates introduce spyware, enabling long-term surveillance.

Notable Campaigns: Lessons from the Frontlines

The annals of cyber espionage are rife with examples of successful phishing campaigns, each illustrating the tactic's adaptability and impact.

1. The Office of Personnel Management (OPM) Breach (2015):

A phishing attack on the U.S. Office of Personnel Management compromised the personal information of over 22 million individuals, including federal employees and military personnel. The breach underscored phishing's ability to bypass robust defences by targeting human weaknesses.

2. APT29 and Cozy Bear:

Associated with Russian intelligence, the Advanced Persistent Threat (APT) group APT29 has used phishing extensively in campaigns targeting governmental and research organisations. In 2020, the group attempted to steal COVID-19 vaccine research through spear-phishing emails laden with malware.

3. Operation Cloud Hopper:

A long-running campaign attributed to Chinese threat actors, Cloud Hopper used phishing to infiltrate managed service providers (MSPs) and, through them, the networks of multiple Fortune 500 companies. The attackers accessed trade secrets, intellectual property, and confidential communications.

The Psychological Arsenal of Espionage Phishing

Phishing in espionage exploits the human psyche as much as it does technological gaps. Its success hinges on carefully crafted psychological triggers:

1. Fear and Authority:

Emails impersonating senior officials or urgent government notices compel recipients to act without question. A directive from the "Minister of Defense" or a "National Security Alert" email creates a sense of immediacy that overrides caution.

2. Curiosity and Greed:

Promises of classified documents, insider information, or lucrative contracts play on natural human curiosity. A "Top Secret Briefing.pdf" attachment is irresistible to even the most cautious recipients.

3. Trust and Familiarity:

Espionage campaigns often impersonate trusted contacts. An email appearing to be from a colleague discussing an ongoing project feels legitimate, encouraging engagement without scrutiny.

The Broader Implications of Phishing in Espionage

The ramifications of phishing-driven espionage extend far beyond the immediate breach, impacting national security, economic stability, and global geopolitics.

1. Compromised National Security:

   Infiltration of government agencies can expose classified operations, jeopardise defence strategies, and endanger lives. Espionage campaigns targeting military contractors or intelligence agencies can disrupt national security frameworks.

2. Economic Espionage:

   Corporations are increasingly targeted by nation-state actors seeking to gain competitive advantages. Intellectual property theft, such as patented technologies or trade secrets, undermines innovation and erodes market leadership.

3. Erosion of Trust:

   Repeated phishing attacks undermine public confidence in institutions. Employees grow wary of digital communications, while citizens question the ability of their governments and corporations to protect sensitive information.

Countermeasures: Building Resilience Against Espionage Phishing

Combating phishing in espionage requires a multi-layered approach that combines technology, education, and policy.

1. Advanced Threat Detection:

AI-powered systems can analyse email patterns, flagging anomalies that indicate phishing attempts. Sandboxing technologies ensure suspicious files are tested in isolated environments before being opened.

2. Human-Centric Defenses:

Regular training programs empower individuals to recognise phishing tactics, fostering a culture of vigilance. Simulated phishing campaigns can help organisations assess and improve their defences.

3. Policy and Collaboration:

International cooperation is essential to address the transnational nature of cyber espionage. Shared intelligence, coordinated sanctions, and harmonised cybersecurity standards can deter state-sponsored phishing campaigns.

CHAPTER 9

SHADOWS OF DECEPTION: LESSONS FROM NOTORIOUS PHISHING ATTACKS

Phishing attacks are the quintessential example of how subtle manipulations can lead to catastrophic consequences. Their deceptively simple methodology—crafting messages to exploit human trust—belies the profound disruption they can unleash. Two infamous cases, the Target breach of 2013 and the Sony Pictures hack of 2014, are stark reminders of phishing's devastating power.

The Target Breach: A Tale of Exploitation Through the Back Door

In 2013, Target Corporation, one of the largest retail chains in the United States, became the victim of a phishing attack that compromised the personal and financial data of over 110 million customers. The attack exemplifies how vulnerabilities in third-party systems can serve as entry points for malicious actors.

1. The Method:

The attackers targeted a small HVAC vendor, Fazio Mechanical, with access to Target's network for billing and maintenance purposes. Through a phishing email, they tricked an employee into downloading malware, providing the attackers with the vendor's credentials.

With these credentials, the attackers accessed Target's systems, eventually installing malware on point-of-sale (POS) devices. This enabled them to capture credit and debit card data during transactions, creating one of retail history's most significant data breaches.

2. The Impact:

- Financial Repercussions: Target incurred over $200 million in legal settlements, security upgrades, and compensation expenses.

- Reputational Damage: Customer trust eroded as the public questioned Target's ability to protect sensitive information.

- Regulatory Fallout: The breach prompted increased scrutiny of cybersecurity practices across the retail sector, highlighting the risks of third-party access.

3. Lessons Learned:

The Target breach underscored the importance of securing supply chain access and implementing strict network segmentation. Advanced detection systems and regular audits of third-party vendors became critical priorities for businesses.

The Sony Pictures Hack: Phishing Meets Geopolitical Drama

The 2014 Sony Pictures hack was a phishing attack wrapped in the intrigue of geopolitical tensions. Orchestrated by the Lazarus Group, a hacking collective linked to North Korea, the attack targeted Sony's internal systems, leaking sensitive data and paralysing operations.

1. The Method:

The attackers used spear-phishing emails tailored to Sony employees, masquerading as legitimate communications. Once recipients engaged with the emails, the malware was deployed, giving the hackers access to Sony's network.

The attackers exfiltrated terabytes of data, including unreleased films, confidential emails, and employees' personal information. They also deployed wiper malware, rendering critical systems inoperable.

2. The Impact:

- Cultural and Political Shockwaves: The hackers released sensitive internal communications, exposing workplace gossip and controversial decisions. This led to public embarrassment for Sony and strained relationships within the organisation.

- Operational Chaos: Sony's systems were crippled, delaying projects and causing significant financial losses.

- Geopolitical Implications: The attack allegedly responded to Sony's production of The Interview, a satirical film about North Korea's leadership. It highlighted the intersection of cybersecurity and international relations.

3. Lessons Learned:

The Sony hack demonstrated the dangers of spear-phishing and the need for robust internal security measures, including employee training, encrypted communications, and advanced threat monitoring. It also emphasised the broader stakes of cybersecurity in an era where digital attacks can serve political objectives.

The Broader Implications of Phishing

These high-profile attacks reveal the multifaceted impact of phishing, extending beyond immediate financial losses to broader societal, organisational, and geopolitical consequences.

1. Erosion of Trust:

Both Target and Sony suffered significant reputational damage, demonstrating how phishing can undermine customer, employee, and stakeholder trust.

2. Economic Consequences:

The financial fallout from phishing attacks extends far beyond direct losses. Legal battles, regulatory fines, and rebuilding systems' costs drain resources that could otherwise fuel growth.

3. Systemic Vulnerabilities:

These incidents exposed weaknesses in how businesses manage third-party access, internal communications, and network security. The ripple effects often trigger industry-wide reforms, pushing organisations to adopt more rigorous standards.

4. The Human Factor:

Phishing exploits human psychology despite technological advancements—curiosity, urgency, and trust. This highlights the enduring importance of employee awareness and training in combating cyber threats.

Evolving Strategies to Counter Phishing

As phishing attacks become more sophisticated, so must the defences against them. Businesses and governments can take proactive measures to mitigate the risk:

1. Advanced Threat Detection:

AI-driven tools can analyse email patterns and detect anomalies indicative of phishing. Behavioral analytics help identify unusual access attempts.

2. Regular Training:

Simulated phishing campaigns can educate employees on recognising red flags, such as suspicious links, unfamiliar sender addresses, and urgent demands.

3. Zero-Trust Architecture:

Implementing a zero-trust model ensures that all internal and external users are continuously authenticated and monitored, minimising the risk of lateral movement within networks.

4. Global Collaboration:

Cybersecurity is a shared responsibility. Governments and organisations must collaborate to share intelligence, establish regulatory frameworks, and coordinate responses to phishing campaigns.

CHAPTER 10

DUAL-EDGED INNOVATION: ARTIFICIAL INTELLIGENCE IN PHISHING AND ITS DETECTION

In the labyrinth of cyberspace, where trust is the currency and deception a lurking shadow, artificial intelligence (AI) emerges as both a formidable ally and a cunning adversary. The evolution of phishing scams has been inexorably linked to technological progress, with AI transforming the threat landscape. On one hand, AI enables the creation of more sophisticated and personalised phishing attacks, making deception nearly indistinguishable from authenticity. Conversely, it powers advanced detection systems that fortify defences against such attacks.

AI-Driven Phishing: A Masterclass in Deception

The sophistication of modern phishing attacks owes much to AI's capabilities in automating, refining, and personalising deception. Gone are the days of generic "Nigerian prince" emails. Today's phishing scams leverage

AI to exploit human psychology with unparalleled precision.

1. Hyper-Personalisation through Data Mining:

AI-powered algorithms comb through vast amounts of publicly available data, including social media profiles, professional networks, and leaked datasets. By synthesising this information, attackers craft messages that resonate personally with their targets.

- Example: A corporate employee might receive a meticulously tailored email from what appears to be their CEO, referencing recent meetings or specific projects. The message's authenticity creates a false sense of trust, increasing the likelihood of compliance.

2. Natural Language Processing (NLP) for Realism:

AI-driven NLP models generate phishing emails with flawless grammar, tone, and context. These messages mimic the style of trusted entities, eliminating the red flags traditionally associated with phishing attempts.

- Advancement: ChatGPT-like systems can compose dynamic, context-aware messages that adapt to ongoing conversations, making detection even harder.

3. Deepfake Technology in Spear Phishing:

AI's ability to generate realistic audio and video deepfakes adds another layer of sophistication. Attackers can impersonate executives in video calls or voice messages, compelling employees to transfer funds or disclose sensitive information.

4. Automated Attack Campaigns:

AI facilitates the automation of large-scale phishing campaigns. Machine learning algorithms optimise these campaigns by analysing recipient behaviour, identifying the most effective methods, and adapting real-time tactics.

The Role of AI in Phishing Detection: A Technological Counterbalance

While AI is a tool for attackers, it is also the cornerstone of modern phishing detection and prevention systems. The same capabilities that enhance phishing are being harnessed to counteract its threats.

1. Behavioural Analysis:

AI-powered systems monitor user behaviour, identifying anomalies that may indicate phishing. For instance, a sudden login attempt from an unusual location or device triggers an alert, preventing unauthorised access.

- Machine Learning Models: These models learn to distinguish between legitimate and malicious activities by analysing vast datasets of historical behaviour.

2. Content Analysis:

AI-driven NLP tools scrutinise emails for signs of phishing, such as suspicious links, manipulated sender details, and unnatural language patterns.

- Example: Advanced spam filters analyse message metadata and content, flagging high-risk emails before they reach users.

3. Phishing Simulations and Training:

AI aids in creating realistic phishing simulations to train employees. By mimicking evolving attack strategies, these simulations improve awareness and resilience.

4. Real-Time Threat Intelligence:

AI systems aggregate and analyse threat data from global networks, identifying emerging phishing campaigns and updating defences accordingly. This proactive approach reduces response times and mitigates damage.

Ethical Considerations and the Arms Race

The use of AI in phishing raises profound ethical questions, particularly regarding the fine line between innovation and misuse.

1. The Democratisation of AI Tools:

Many AI tools, including deepfake generators and NLP models, are freely available, enabling malicious actors to exploit them. The challenge lies in balancing accessibility with safeguards against misuse.

2. The Escalation of the Cyber Arms Race:

AI's continuous advancement in offensive and defensive capacities creates a cyclical arms race. Attackers develop more sophisticated methods, prompting defenders to enhance detection technologies, perpetuating an unending cycle of escalation.

3. Accountability and Regulation:

Governments and organisations must grapple with questions of accountability. Who bears responsibility when AI-generated phishing scams cause harm? How can we regulate the use of AI without stifling innovation?

The Broader Implications of AI-Driven Phishing

Integrating AI into phishing and its detection has far-reaching implications for individuals, businesses, and society.

1. Erosion of Trust in Digital Communication:

As phishing becomes more challenging to detect, trust in digital communication channels erodes.

Users grow wary of emails, messages, and even video calls, complicating workflows and relationships.

2. Economic Costs:

AI-driven phishing scams amplify financial losses. Businesses face direct theft and the costs of remediation, legal battles, and reputational damage.

3. Psychological Impact:

Victims of AI-enhanced phishing experience heightened feelings of betrayal and insecurity. The realism of these attacks can make them feel deeply personal, compounding emotional distress.

4. The Necessity of Cyber Literacy:

The evolving threat landscape underscores the importance of cyber literacy. Users must understand the capabilities of AI-driven attacks and adopt a proactive mindset to mitigate risks.

CHAPTER 11

UNMASKING DECEPTION: A GUIDE TO IDENTIFYING PHISHING ATTEMPTS THROUGH URL VERIFICATION, EMAIL HEADERS, AND SECURITY TOOLS

In a world increasingly defined by digital interactions, the line between trust and treachery has grown perilously thin. Phishing, a cybercrime that preys on human vulnerability, has become a ubiquitous threat. While it masquerades as legitimate communication, its goal is nefarious: to steal sensitive information, compromise accounts, or install malicious software. Protecting oneself against phishing is no longer optional but essential.

The First Line of Defense: URL Verification

Every phishing attempt begins with deception, often

hidden within a seemingly innocuous URL. Scrutinising web addresses is vital in identifying and thwarting phishing attacks.

1. Recognising Malicious Links:

URLs in phishing emails often mimic legitimate ones but include subtle alterations. For example, "www.paypa1.com" replaces the letter "l" with the numeral "1," or "secure-payments.com" might be unrelated to the actual PayPal domain.

- Tips for Verification:
  - Hover, Don't Click: Always hover over a link to preview its destination. Most email clients and browsers display the URL in the bottom-left corner.
  - Inspect Closely: Look for misspellings, extra characters, or unusual extensions (e.g., ".ru" instead of ".com").
  - Use Trusted Tools: Tools like VirusTotal or Google's Safe Browsing Transparency Report can analyse URLs for signs of phishing.

2. The Rise of HTTPS Confusion:

The presence of "https://" does not guarantee a site

is safe. Cybercriminals exploit free SSL certificates to give their fraudulent websites an air of legitimacy.

- Understanding Certificates: Use browser features to view SSL certificate details. Check if the certificate matches the organisation it claims to represent.

3. Shortened URLs and QR Codes:

Attackers often use URL shorteners or QR codes to obscure malicious links. Tools like CheckShortURL can expand and analyse shortened links, while QR code scanners with built-in safety features can help verify hidden destinations.

Cracking the Code: Email Header Analysis

An email header is a treasure trove of information that, when deciphered, can reveal the authenticity of an email. While often overlooked, email headers hold clues that expose phishing attempts.

1. Understanding Email Headers:

Every email has a header containing metadata such as the sender's IP address, the mail server path, and the authentication status. Accessing this information requires technical know-how but can be invaluable.

- How to View Headers:
  - In Gmail: Click the three

dots in the email's top-right corner and select "Show original."

- In Outlook: Right-click the email, choose "Properties," and look for the "Internet headers" section.

2. Key Indicators of Phishing:

- Sender's Domain: Check if the sender's domain matches the organisation they claim to represent. A phishing email may originate from "support@paypa1.com" instead of "support@paypal.com."

- Received Paths: Look for discrepancies in the path the email took. Legitimate emails usually have fewer hops between trusted servers.

- SPF, DKIM, and DMARC Failures: These email authentication protocols help verify the sender's identity. Emails that fail these checks are likely fraudulent.

3. Practical Tools:

Online parsers like MxToolBox can analyse email headers and highlight red flags, such as mismatched sender addresses or suspicious IP origins.

Fortifying Vigilance: Leveraging Security Tools

Technology plays a pivotal role in complementing human vigilance. Security tools act as a safety net, identifying and blocking phishing attempts before they cause harm.

1. Anti-Phishing Browser Extensions:

Extensions like Avast Online Security or Norton Safe Web provide real-time warnings about suspicious websites, protecting users as they browse.

2. Email Security Filters:

Advanced spam filters, powered by machine learning, automatically flag potential phishing emails.

- Customising Filters: Users can enhance their filters by marking suspicious emails as spam, helping the system learn and improve over time.

3. Password Managers:

Password managers can prevent phishing by auto-filling credentials only on verified websites. If a malicious site attempts to mimic a legitimate one, the manager will not recognise it and refuse to populate the fields.

4. Multi-Factor Authentication (MFA):

MFA adds a layer of security. Even if a phishing attempt succeeds in stealing a password, the lack of a secondary authentication factor can render the stolen credentials useless.

5. Threat Intelligence Platforms:

Tools like Proofpoint or Barracuda aggregate global threat data to detect and neutralise phishing campaigns before they reach users.

Empowering Vigilance: A Cultural Shift

While technical defences are essential, fostering a culture of cyber awareness is equally critical. Phishing thrives on ignorance; education is its antidote.

1. Phishing Awareness Training:

Regular training sessions help individuals recognise and respond to phishing attempts. Realistic simulations test users' ability to identify threats, reinforcing their knowledge.

2. Promoting a "Trust but Verify" Mindset:

Encouraging scepticism towards unsolicited communications can reduce impulsive responses to phishing attempts. Users should verify unexpected requests through independent channels, especially those involving sensitive information or financial transactions.

3. Building a Support Network:

Organisations should establish clear protocols for reporting suspicious emails, creating a collective defence against phishing.

CHAPTER 12

BUILDING A RESILIENT DIGITAL FRONTIER: THE IMPERATIVE OF CYBERSECURITY EDUCATION

In a world where the boundaries of digital and physical blur, the need for cybersecurity has transcended technical jargon to become a fundamental life skill. Everyone is a potential target in an age dominated by sophisticated cyber threats, from multinational corporations to individual users navigating social media. The solution lies in robust software defences and individuals' empowered, informed actions. Cybersecurity education is no longer optional; it is a necessity.

Cybersecurity Education: The Shield Against Modern Threats

The growing complexity of cyberattacks, from phishing and ransomware to advanced persistent threats (APTs), demands an equally sophisticated response. Education equips users with the tools to recognise, resist, and respond to cyber threats.

1. The Human Element in Cybersecurity:

According to studies, human error accounts for over 80% of data breaches. Clicking a malicious link, using weak passwords, or failing to update software are actions that hackers exploit. Cybersecurity education addresses these vulnerabilities by fostering a culture of awareness.

2. Bridging the Knowledge Gap:

As cyber threats evolve, so must our understanding of them. Education closes the knowledge gap between attackers and potential victims, transforming users from liabilities into assets in the fight against cybercrime.

Effective Training Programs: Learning from Examples

The efficacy of cybersecurity education lies in its practical application and adaptability to diverse audiences. Several training programs exemplify how education can be both impactful and engaging.

1. Cybersecurity Awareness Month (CSAM):

Initiated by the U.S. Department of Homeland Security, CSAM promotes awareness through workshops, webinars, and campaigns tailored to individuals and businesses. Its themes, such as "See Yourself in Cyber," emphasise personal responsibility and actionable steps to enhance online safety.

2. Phishing Simulations:

Companies like Proofpoint and KnowBe4 conduct phishing simulations as part of their training programs. Employees receive mock phishing emails designed to mimic real-world threats. Those who fall for the traps receive immediate feedback and additional training.

- Impact: Research shows a significant reduction in susceptibility to phishing attacks among employees who undergo such training.

3. Cybersecurity Games and Gamification:

Organisations like CyberPatriot (a youth program run by the Air Force Association) use competitive games to teach cybersecurity concepts. Participants learn to secure networks, manage vulnerabilities, and identify threats in a simulated environment.

- Why It Works: Gamification turns learning into an interactive, enjoyable experience, increasing retention and engagement.

4. National Cybersecurity Institutes:

Institutions like SANS Institute offer comprehensive courses for professionals, ranging from entry-level to advanced certifications. Their hands-on labs, real-time threat analysis, and collaborative projects prepare participants for the dynamic nature of cybersecurity.

The Role of Organisations in Promoting Cybersecurity Education

Organisations serve as both targets and protectors in the cybersecurity ecosystem. Their role in fostering education is paramount.

1. Mandatory Training Programs:

Leading corporations like IBM and Microsoft mandate cybersecurity training for all employees, regardless of role.

- Benefits: Such initiatives ensure that every employee, from the intern to the CEO, understands the basics of cybersecurity.

2. Tailored Education:

Effective training programs are customised to fit the specific needs of an organisation. For instance:

- Healthcare: Focus on HIPAA compliance and patient data protection.
- Finance: Emphasis on detecting fraud and securing transactions.

3. Continuous Learning:

Cybersecurity is not a one-time lesson but an ongoing process. Regular updates, refreshers, and workshops inform employees about the latest threats and technologies.

4. Empowering IT Teams:

Specialised training for IT and security teams ensures they can handle advanced threats like zero-day exploits and APTs.

The Ripple Effect: Individual Empowerment

While organisations play a crucial role, individual users must also take ownership of their cybersecurity education. The ripple effect of informed individuals extends to families, communities, and workplaces.

1. Digital Hygiene Practices:

Cybersecurity education teaches essential but vital practices, such as:

- Use strong, unique passwords for each account.
- Enabling multi-factor authentication (MFA).
- Avoiding public Wi-Fi for sensitive transactions.

2. Youth and Cybersecurity:

Including cybersecurity in school curricula prepares the next generation for the challenges of a digital-first world. Initiatives like Google's "Be Internet Awesome" teach children how to navigate the internet safely and responsibly.

3. Empowering Vulnerable Groups:

Education targeted at seniors, who are often the victims of scams, and small business owners, who may lack IT resources, addresses critical gaps in awareness and protection.

A Collaborative Future

The battle against cyber threats is not one that individuals, organisations, or governments can fight alone. Cybersecurity education thrives in a collaborative ecosystem.

1. Public-Private Partnerships:

Initiatives like the Cybersecurity and Infrastructure Security Agency's (CISA) programs bring together governments, businesses, and academia to promote education and share resources.

2. Global Outreach:

Programs like Cyber4Dev aim to strengthen cybersecurity education in developing nations, recognising that a secure internet benefits everyone.

3. Leveraging Technology:

Artificial intelligence and machine learning are integrated into education tools to create personalised learning experiences, identify knowledge gaps, and predict emerging threats.

CHAPTER 13

NAVIGATING THE LEGAL AND ETHICAL MAZE: COMBATING PHISHING IN THE DIGITAL AGE

In cyberspace's vast, boundless terrain, phishing operates like a shadowy spectre, exploiting technological vulnerabilities and human trust. As the digital age progresses, society finds itself grappling not just with technical defences but also with the intricacies of legal and ethical challenges in combating phishing.

Legal Frameworks: The Patchwork of Global Efforts

Phishing, by its nature, transcends borders. An email crafted in one country can victimise individuals in another, rendering traditional legal approaches inadequate. Addressing phishing requires a synchronised global response, yet the legal landscape remains fragmented.

1. International Legal Disparities:

The absence of a universally binding legal framework to combat phishing creates enforcement challenges. Different nations impose varying penalties, definitions, and thresholds for cybercrimes:

- Example: While the United States enforces laws like the Computer Fraud and Abuse Act (CFAA) to prosecute phishing attacks, other nations may lack equivalent legislation or resources, making extradition and cross-border prosecution complex.

2. The Role of International Agreements:

Instruments like the Budapest Convention on Cybercrime provide a foundation for international cooperation. Signatory countries agree to criminalise offences like phishing and assist each other in investigations. However, non-signatory nations, including major players like China and Russia, limit its effectiveness.

3. Emerging Regional Initiatives:

Regional collaborations, such as the European Union's General Data Protection Regulation (GDPR), aim to secure personal data, indirectly deterring phishing. GDPR mandates stringent penalties for companies failing to protect user data, thus encouraging better cybersecurity practices.

Jurisdictional Challenges: Who Has the Authority?

Phishing raises profound jurisdictional questions, mainly when perpetrators operate in one country while targeting victims in another.

1. Conflict of Laws:

A phishing attack from a country with lax cybercrime laws may leave victims with little recourse. For example:

- A victim in Germany falls prey to a phishing scheme orchestrated in a jurisdiction where cybercrime is not rigorously prosecuted. Efforts to hold the attacker accountable can stall in the face of bureaucratic and legal roadblocks.

2. Cloud Computing and Data Jurisdiction:

Phishing often exploits cloud infrastructure. Determining jurisdiction over stolen data stored in international cloud servers complicates enforcement efforts, as varying laws govern data ownership and access.

3. Case Study: The 2017 Yahoo Data Breach

Hackers who orchestrated the breach leveraged jurisdictional gaps to evade authorities for years. Cooperation between U.S. and Canadian law enforcement eventually led to arrests, underscoring the critical need for international collaboration.

Ethical Challenges: Striking the Balance

The fight against phishing is a legal issue and an ethical tightrope walk where the lines between security and personal freedom blur.

1. Privacy vs. Surveillance:

   - Governments and corporations often deploy advanced monitoring tools to detect phishing schemes. However, these measures can infringe on individual privacy rights, raising ethical concerns.

   - Example: Monitoring email content for phishing indicators can inadvertently expose personal communications, challenging the principle of data confidentiality.

2. Honeypots and Ethical Boundaries:

Law enforcement agencies sometimes create "honeypots" — fake systems to attract phishers and gather evidence. While effective, this strategy raises questions about entrapment and whether it crosses ethical boundaries by baiting criminals into committing offences.

3. Corporate Responsibility:

Organisations face ethical dilemmas in disclosing

phishing-related breaches. Many opt to suppress information to protect their reputation, leaving customers vulnerable. Ethical governance mandates transparency, yet the fear of financial and reputational damage often trumps moral obligations.

Legislative Innovations: The Way Forward

Innovative legislation can address legal gaps and ethical concerns, paving the way for more effective anti-phishing measures.

1. Data Protection Laws:

Strengthening data protection frameworks worldwide can deter phishing by making it harder for attackers to access sensitive information. Laws like California's Consumer Privacy Act (CCPA) empower individuals with greater control over their data, limiting opportunities for exploitation.

2. Mandatory Reporting of Cyber Incidents:

Governments can mandate timely reporting of phishing incidents to enhance transparency and foster a culture of accountability. For instance:

- The United Kingdom's National Cyber Security Centre (NCSC) encourages businesses to report phishing campaigns, providing data that aids collective defences.

3. Global Cybersecurity Alliances:

Expanding the scope and participation of international alliances can facilitate information sharing and joint operations against phishing syndicates. Collaborative exercises, such as Interpol's Operation Night Fury, demonstrate the potential of unified efforts in dismantling phishing networks.

A Collaborative Ethical Vision

Beyond laws and policies, combating phishing requires a shared ethical vision emphasising collective responsibility.

1. Public-Private Partnerships:

Governments and corporations must work together to create secure digital ecosystems. Companies like Google and Microsoft have taken proactive steps by integrating phishing detection tools into their platforms. Collaborative efforts can amplify these initiatives, fostering trust and shared accountability.

2. Empowering Individuals:

Ethical cybersecurity education empowers users to protect themselves while respecting their rights —initiatives like the STOP. THINK. CONNECT. Campaigns exemplify how governments can promote awareness without infringing on privacy.

3. Ethics in Technology Design:

Technology companies bear a moral obligation to prioritise security in their designs. From two-factor authentication to AI-driven phishing detection, ethical considerations must underpin every innovation.

CHAPTER 14

A SHIELD AGAINST DECEPTION: PRACTICAL STEPS AND SOLUTIONS FOR COMBATTING PHISHING

In the vast and ever-evolving digital landscape, phishing is the invisible predator, preying on trust, curiosity, and fear. The consequences of falling victim to phishing are dire: financial losses, identity theft, and the erosion of confidence in the digital world. Yet, amidst the complexity of this threat lies a beacon of hope—practical steps and technological solutions that empower individuals and organisations to guard against phishing and recover swiftly if compromised.

Understanding the Threat: The Foundation of Prevention

Before diving into solutions, it is crucial to grasp the anatomy of a phishing attack. Phishing thrives on human error, leveraging social engineering to deceive individuals into revealing sensitive information. Attackers craft deceptive emails, messages, or websites, exploiting emotions like fear, urgency, and greed. Recognising these tactics is the first step toward effective prevention.

Practical Steps for Individuals

1. Develop a Critical Eye:

Vigilance is the most powerful tool in combating phishing. This involves scrutinising communications for common signs of deception:

- Check the sender's address: Legitimate organisations rarely use generic email domains.

- Inspect links: Hover over URLs to reveal their true destination.

- Watch for urgency: Phishing messages often pressure recipients into hasty decisions.

2. Strengthen Digital Hygiene:

- Enable two-factor authentication (2FA): This adds a layer of security, making it harder for attackers to access accounts even if credentials are stolen.

- Use unique, strong passwords: Employ a password manager to securely generate and store complex passwords.

- Keep software updated: Regular updates patch vulnerabilities that phishing campaigns often exploit.

3. Leverage Awareness Campaigns:

Governments and organisations provide valuable resources to educate the public through campaigns like STOP. THINK. CONNECT. Encourage users to pause and assess before clicking suspicious links.

Technological Solutions for Organisations

1. Email Filtering and Security Tools:

  - Spam filters: Advanced email filters use machine learning to identify and block phishing emails.

  - Secure Email Gateways (SEGs): These tools inspect incoming and outgoing emails, identifying threats like fake URLs and attachments laden with malware.

2. Endpoint Detection and Response (EDR):

Organisations can deploy EDR systems to monitor endpoints (e.g., employee computers) for suspicious activities and respond promptly to threats.

3. Phishing Simulation and Training:

  - Regular simulation exercises can test employees' ability to recognise phishing attempts, reinforcing good habits.

  - Gamified training platforms make cybersecurity learning engaging and memorable, promoting better retention of key concepts.

4. Domain-based Message Authentication, Reporting, and Conformance (DMARC):

DMARC is a protocol that authenticates the sender's domain, preventing attackers from spoofing legitimate email addresses.

Responding to Phishing: Swift Action to Minimise Damage

Even with robust preventive measures, incidents can occur. Knowing how to respond effectively can limit the fallout.

1. Immediate Steps for Individuals:

   - Disconnect from the network: Disconnecting can prevent further damage if you suspect a phishing link installed malware.

   - Change passwords: Update all credentials, especially those tied to the compromised account.

   - Enable account recovery: Use recovery options to regain control of accounts and lock out the attacker.

2. Incident Response for Organisations:

   - Isolate-affected systems: Contain the breach to prevent its spread.

- Activate the incident response plan: Every organisation should have a pre-defined strategy for managing phishing-related incidents.

- Conduct forensic analysis: Understanding the scope of the attack aids in mitigation and future prevention.

- Communicate transparently: Notify affected stakeholders promptly, detailing the steps to resolve the issue.

3. Reporting Phishing:

- To authorities: Reporting to cybersecurity agencies like the Cybersecurity and Infrastructure Security Agency (CISA) or local equivalents aids collective defences.

- To email providers: Marking emails as phishing helps providers improve their filtering algorithms.

The Human Factor: A Collective Responsibility

While technology is essential, the human factor remains pivotal in the fight against phishing. Encouraging a culture of vigilance and responsibility is key:

- For individuals: Cultivate curiosity and scepticism about unsolicited communications.

- For organisations: Foster open communication, where employees feel comfortable reporting suspicious activities without fear of reprimand.

Innovative Tools for a Phishing-Resilient Future

1. Artificial Intelligence (AI) in Detection:

AI-driven solutions analyse patterns in phishing attempts, adapting to evolving tactics. These tools can process vast amounts of data to identify threats with unparalleled accuracy.

2. Browser Protections:

Modern browsers like Chrome and Firefox integrate phishing protection features, warning users before they access known malicious sites.

3. Blockchain for Verification:

Blockchain technology offers the potential for creating tamper-proof systems that verify the authenticity of communications, adding another layer of defence.

CHAPTER 15

BEHIND THE VEIL: THE DARK WEB'S ROLE IN ENABLING PHISHING

Beneath the surface of the internet lies a shadowy underworld: the dark web. It is shrouded in mystery, often evoking images of secretive exchanges, illicit markets, and untraceable anonymity. While not inherently malicious, the dark web has become a fertile ground for criminal activity, and among its most insidious offerings is its role in facilitating phishing attacks. By providing cybercriminals with tools, templates, and platforms, the dark web enables phishing schemes that exploit the vulnerabilities of our increasingly digital lives.

A Hidden Ecosystem of Crime

The dark web operates on encrypted networks, most commonly through software like Tor (The Onion Router), which conceals users' identities and locations. While essential for privacy advocates and whistleblowers, this anonymity also shields malicious actors. Within this clandestine environment, a thriving marketplace exists where phishing kits, fake websites, and stolen credentials are bought and sold.

Unlike the stereotypical image of a lone hacker, phishing campaigns today are often the result of coordinated efforts supported by the dark web's infrastructure. It functions as a supply chain, streamlining the creation and execution of phishing attacks with unprecedented precision.

Phishing Kits and Templates: Lowering the Barrier to Entry

One of the dark web's most significant contributions to phishing is the proliferation of phishing kits—prepackaged tools that simplify the creation of fake websites and emails. These kits typically include:

- Templates: Precise replicas of legitimate websites, such as banking portals or e-commerce platforms.
- Scripts: Automated scripts to harvest and store victims' credentials.
- Guides: Step-by-step instructions for deploying phishing campaigns.

Such kits are marketed to even the least tech-savvy individuals, democratising cybercrime. For instance, a novice with minimal technical expertise can purchase a phishing kit that mimics a primary online payment service, customise it with stolen branding, and launch an attack within hours.

Stolen Data Markets

The dark web is also the marketplace where the fruits of phishing are monetised. Credentials harvested through phishing schemes—such as email addresses, passwords, or credit card details—are sold in bulk. These data bundles often include "extras," such as IP addresses and geographic information, which allow buyers to bypass fraud detection systems.

Prices on these illicit markets vary depending on the quality and quantity of the data. For instance:

- Email credentials with verified access to business accounts fetch higher prices than generic consumer email accounts.

- "Fullz" packages (comprehensive identity records, including Social Security numbers and financial details) are among the most valuable.

This commodification of stolen data underscores the industrial scale of phishing operations facilitated by the dark web.

Anonymity and the Tools of Deception

Anonymity is the dark web's cornerstone, and cybercriminals exploit it to conduct their activities without fear of detection. Tools like cryptocurrency —especially privacy-focused coins such as Monero— enable untraceable transactions, ensuring that financial exchanges remain hidden.

Additionally, the dark web offers:

- Bulletproof hosting services: Servers in jurisdictions with lax regulations resist takedowns or legal actions.

- Anonymising technologies: Tools to obscure the origins of phishing emails, making it nearly impossible for victims or authorities to trace their source.

These elements create an environment where phishing campaigns can thrive unchecked, evolving in sophistication and scope.

Collaboration and Skill Sharing

The dark web is not merely a marketplace but a hub of collaboration and learning for cybercriminals. Forums and chat rooms serve as virtual classrooms where experienced attackers share insights, discuss strategies, and troubleshoot technical challenges. Topics often include:

- Circumventing spam filters: Techniques to ensure phishing emails bypass sophisticated detection systems.

- Social engineering tactics: Psychological methods to manipulate victims into divulging sensitive information.

- Exploiting current events: Leveraging global crises or trends (e.g., pandemics or tax season) to craft convincing phishing narratives.

Such exchanges accelerate the evolution of phishing tactics, making them harder to detect and combat.

The Ethical and Legal Conundrum

The dark web's role in phishing raises complex ethical and legal questions. While its anonymity can protect whistleblowers and activists in oppressive regimes, the exact mechanisms empower cybercriminals. Efforts to police the dark web often result in collateral damage, disrupting legitimate uses of its technology.

Moreover, international jurisdiction complicates enforcement. Phishing campaigns launched through dark web services may involve actors, victims, and infrastructure spread across multiple countries, creating significant legal and logistical challenges.

Combatting the Dark Web's Influence

Addressing the dark web's role in phishing requires a multifaceted approach:

1. Enhanced Monitoring and Intelligence:

Law enforcement agencies are increasingly deploying AI-driven tools to monitor dark web activities. By infiltrating forums and marketplaces, investigators can gather intelligence on phishing operations and identify key players.

2. Disrupting Infrastructure:

Collaborative international efforts, such as Europol's takedowns of dark web marketplaces, aim to dismantle the platforms that enable phishing campaigns.

3. Raising Awareness:

Public education campaigns must emphasise the risks of phishing and the dark web, equipping individuals with the knowledge to protect themselves.

4. Regulating Cryptocurrency:

Strengthening regulations around cryptocurrency transactions can limit the financial anonymity that fuels dark web marketplaces.

CHAPTER 16

NAVIGATING THE FUTURE OF DECEPTION: EMERGING PHISHING TECHNIQUES AND THE EVOLUTION OF CYBERSECURITY

In the endless dance between offence and defence, phishing remains one of the most dynamic threats in the cybersecurity landscape. No longer limited to crude emails riddled with spelling errors, phishing has evolved into a sophisticated ecosystem, adapting to technological advancements and exploiting human vulnerabilities with precision. As the digital world transforms through innovations like artificial intelligence (AI), machine learning, and quantum computing, phishing techniques are also becoming more insidious.

The New Face of Phishing: Techniques of Tomorrow

Phishing, in its essence, is the art of deception. It thrives on exploiting trust, urgency, and fear. Emerging techniques reflect an unsettling refinement of these tactics, blending psychological manipulation with cutting-edge technology.

1. Deepfake Phishing

Deepfake technology, which leverages AI to create convincing audio and video forgeries, is rapidly becoming a tool for cybercriminals. Imagine receiving a video call from your CEO asking for sensitive information or an urgent wire transfer—only to discover later that it was an AI-generated illusion. This attack capitalises on visual and auditory cues that were once considered reliable markers of authenticity.

2. Context-Aware Phishing

Traditional phishing campaigns often rely on generic messages, but emerging attacks are becoming hyper-personalised. Cybercriminals craft messages that resonate with their targets' lives by Leveraging data from social media leaked credentials or public records. A phishing email about a charity drive for a cause you recently supported or a fake invoice for a service you used is far harder to ignore.

3. Multi-Vector Phishing

Gone are the days when phishing was limited to email. Cybercriminals now employ multi-vector attacks that span email, SMS (smishing), voice calls (Vishing), and social media. A single campaign might involve an initial phishing email followed by a vishing call to confirm "details," creating a layered deception that increases the likelihood of success.

The Role of Evolving Technologies in Phishing

The technologies driving the next wave of innovation also empower cybercriminals, making phishing attacks more pervasive and difficult to detect.

Artificial Intelligence and Machine Learning

AI is a double-edged sword in cybersecurity. While defenders use it to identify anomalies and automate threat detection, attackers exploit it to craft convincing phishing content. Machine learning algorithms can analyse massive datasets to determine effective tactics, generate realistic emails, and adapt in real time to evade detection.

Natural Language Processing (NLP)

NLP enables phishing messages to mimic human language with remarkable fluency. Advanced models can create emails free of the grammatical errors and awkward phrasing that once served as red flags. More disturbingly, they can tailor tone and style to match the victim's expectations, such as replicating the casual style of a colleague or the formality of an official request.

Quantum Computing

While still in its infancy, quantum computing poses a potential game-changer for phishing and cybersecurity. In theory, the sheer computational power of quantum systems could be used to crack encryption algorithms that secure communication channels, opening new avenues for phishing attacks.

The Adaptation of Cybersecurity

To counter the evolving phishing landscape, cybersecurity must evolve in parallel, embracing innovation while reinforcing fundamental defences.

1. Behavioral Analytics and AI-Powered Defenses

AI isn't just a tool for attackers; it's a cornerstone of modern cybersecurity. Behavioural analytics, powered by machine learning, can identify unusual patterns in user activity, such as logging in from unfamiliar locations or executing abnormal transactions. Combined with AI-driven email filters, this approach significantly reduces the risk of successful phishing attempts.

2. Zero-Trust Architecture

The zero-trust model, which assumes that every user and device poses a potential threat, is gaining traction as a countermeasure to phishing. Zero-trust systems minimise the damage a successful phishing attack can cause by enforcing strict verification processes at every access point.

3. Cybersecurity Education for the Masses

While technological solutions are vital, human awareness remains a critical line of defence. Cybersecurity education programs must evolve to address emerging phishing techniques, teaching individuals to recognise deepfake content, verify unexpected requests, and adopt secure online behaviours. Gamified training modules and phishing simulations can make learning more engaging and effective.

Challenges in Staying Ahead

The battle against phishing is inherently asymmetrical. Attackers need only to succeed once, while defenders must always be vigilant. Several challenges complicate the adaptation process:

- Rapid Innovation: Technological development's pace means defences are often reactive rather than proactive.

- Resource Disparity: While large corporations can invest in advanced cybersecurity measures, small businesses and individuals often lack the resources to implement robust defences.

- Human Error: Despite training and tools, the innate tendencies of curiosity and trust make humans the weakest link in cybersecurity.

A Call to Action

Phishing is more than a technical problem; it is a societal challenge that demands a collective response. Governments, businesses, and individuals must work together to create a resilient digital ecosystem. This includes:

- Stronger Legislation: Governments must enforce laws that target cybercriminals and regulate technologies that enable phishing.

- Public-Private Partnerships: Collaboration between the public sector and technology companies can accelerate the development of innovative defences.

- Global Cooperation: Phishing knows no borders. International efforts are crucial to dismantle criminal networks and address jurisdictional challenges.

CHAPTER 17

TOWARD A SAFER DIGITAL WORLD: EMBRACING COLLECTIVE RESPONSIBILITY IN THE FIGHT AGAINST PHISHING

The digital age has delivered boundless opportunities, connecting people and ideas like never before. Yet, it has also brought profound challenges, none more insidious than phishing. What began as crude deceptions in the early days of email has evolved into a sophisticated enterprise targeting individuals, businesses, and governments. Phishing isn't merely a technological issue; it's a societal problem that reflects the vulnerabilities of an interconnected world.

The Role of Governments: Frameworks and Enforcement

Governments hold a unique position of authority and influence as the architects of laws and policies protecting citizens in both physical and digital spaces. Yet, the dynamic nature of phishing presents specific challenges that demand innovation and global cooperation.

1. Crafting Effective Legislation

Phishing thrives on jurisdictional loopholes. Cybercriminals often operate from countries with lax enforcement or inadequate legal frameworks, exploiting gaps in international cooperation. Governments must establish comprehensive cybersecurity laws that punish perpetrators and mandate robust defences for critical sectors. Recent legislation, such as the EU's General Data Protection Regulation (GDPR), demonstrates how policy can incentivize organizations to prioritize security.

2. Global Collaboration

Phishing is a borderless crime, requiring a borderless response. Governments must invest in international partnerships, sharing intelligence and resources to dismantle criminal networks. Initiatives like the Budapest Convention on Cybercrime provide a foundation, but more inclusive frameworks are needed to involve nations across all levels of technological development.

3. Public Awareness Campaigns

Governments also play a vital role in education. Public service announcements, school curricula, and community workshops can raise awareness about phishing, empowering citizens with the knowledge to protect themselves.

Corporate Responsibility: Innovation and Vigilance

In the corporate world, the stakes of phishing are exceptionally high. A single successful attack can result in financial losses, data breaches, and irreparable damage to reputation. As such, companies bear significant responsibility in safeguarding their operations and the trust of their customers and employees.

1. Investing in Cybersecurity

No organization is too large—or too small—to fall victim to phishing. Companies must view cybersecurity as a core component of their operations, allocating sufficient resources to develop and implement defences. This includes deploying advanced technologies like artificial intelligence to detect and neutralize threats in real-time.

2. Employee Training and Culture

Humans remain the weakest link in cybersecurity. Even the most advanced systems are vulnerable if employees are unaware of phishing attempts. Companies must cultivate a security culture, offering regular training and simulations to ensure employees remain vigilant. This is particularly important in hybrid and remote work environments, where traditional security perimeters no longer apply.

3. Ethical Technology Development

For technology companies, responsibility extends to the tools they create. Developers of email platforms, social media networks, and communication apps must prioritize user safety, embedding anti-phishing measures into their products. Moreover, companies should take a stand against the misuse of emerging technologies like AI and deepfakes, ensuring cybercriminals do not co-opt them.

Empowering Individuals: The Last Line of Defense

While governments and companies provide the scaffolding of cybersecurity, individuals are the final and most critical line of defence. Every click, download, and interaction contributes to the digital ecosystem's collective security— or vulnerability.

1. Awareness and Education

The adage "knowledge is power" holds in the fight against phishing. Individuals must learn to recognize the red flags of phishing attempts, from suspicious URLs to urgent requests for personal information. Online courses, cybersecurity blogs, and community forums provide accessible resources for self-education.

2. Adopting Best Practices

Simple habits can make a significant difference. Strong, unique passwords, enabling multi-factor authentication, and regularly updating software are small steps that drastically reduce the risk of falling victim to phishing.

3. Reporting and Accountability

When phishing attempts occur, individuals have a

responsibility to report them. Whether notifying an employer's IT department or flagging an email to a service provider, such actions disrupt the cycle of deception and help protect others.

Building a Culture of Shared Responsibility

What unites governments, companies, and individuals in this effort is a shared goal: fostering a culture of cybersecurity. This culture transcends technological measures, focusing instead on trust, vigilance, and accountability. It requires breaking down silos, encouraging collaboration, and recognizing that digital security is a collective endeavour.

The Power of Collective Action

Consider the analogy of a community defending itself against a natural disaster. Individual preparedness, corporate resources, and government coordination are all necessary for survival. Similarly, combating phishing demands a unified front, where each stakeholder plays a role in fortifying the digital landscape.

The Human Element

Amid the complexity of phishing and its technical countermeasures, it is essential to remember the human element. Phishing exploits emotions—fear, greed, curiosity —but it also reveals a more profound truth: that humans, for all their vulnerabilities, possess the capacity to learn, adapt, and innovate. By embracing this capacity, we can transform our weaknesses into strengths.

Conclusion: Toward a Secure Digital Future

The fight against phishing is not a battle fought in isolation but a collective journey toward a safer digital future. Governments must lead with vision and resolve, crafting laws that protect without compromising freedoms. Companies must innovate responsibly, balancing profit with the ethical imperative to safeguard their users. Individuals must embrace their role as active participants, understanding that every informed choice contributes to a more vigorous defence.

In this shared endeavour, the digital world mirrors the real one: no one is immune to risk, but together, we are resilient. By recognizing our interconnectedness and embracing the responsibility it entails, we can turn the tide against phishing, reclaiming the promise of technology as a force for good.

As we close this book on phishing, let it serve not as an ending but as a call to action—a reminder that the strength of our defences lies not in the tools we build but in the trust we foster and the unity we sustain.

ABOUT THE AUTHOR

Dr. Karthik K is a distinguished Computational Fluid Dynamics (CFD) specialist, academician, and author with extensive research, education, and industry background. Holding a Ph.D. and M.S. from IIT Madras, Dr. Karthik has spent over a decade exploring the intricate intersections of technology, science, and human behaviour.

Driven by a passion for unravelling complex challenges, Dr. Karthik has contributed significantly to data analysis, artificial intelligence, and cybersecurity. His academic tenure includes guiding student startups, publishing groundbreaking research, and spearheading innovative projects funded by leading organizations. As an AI Engineer at Prediscan Medtech, he focuses on leveraging advanced technologies to solve real-world problems, including those in the healthcare sector.

Dr. Karthik's journey into cybersecurity stems from his fascination with the dynamics of digital deception and the human vulnerabilities that cybercriminals exploit. With a unique ability to distil intricate technical concepts into engaging narratives, he has authored multiple books and publications that bridge the gap between expert knowledge and accessible learning.

Beyond his professional pursuits, Dr. Karthik advocates for digital literacy and cybersecurity education, believing that an informed society is the first defence against modern cyber threats. Fluent in English, Tamil, and Malayalam, he seamlessly connects with diverse audiences worldwide.

In The Art and Science of Phishing: Understanding, Preventing, and Responding, Dr. Karthik offers a comprehensive guide to one of the most persistent challenges of our digital age. His insights from rigorous research and practical experience empower individuals and organizations to navigate the ever-evolving phishing landscape with confidence and resilience.

Connect with Dr. Karthik on his professional journey at karthikk@alumni.iitm.ac.in.